Copyright 2022 by Dr. Archibald Johar

This document is geared towards providing exact and reliable information in regard to the topic and issue covered. If advice is necessary, legal, or professional, a practiced individual in the profession should be ordered. In no way is it legal to reproduce, duplicate, or transmit any part of this document by either electronic means or in printed format. Recording of this publication is strictly prohibited and any storage of this document is not allowed unless with written permission from the publisher. All rights reserved. The information provided herein is stated to be truthful and consistent, in that any liability, in terms of inattention or otherwise, by any usage or abuse of any policies, processes, or instructions contained within is the solitary and utter responsibility of the recipient reader. Under no circumstances will any legal responsibility or blame be held against the publisher for any reparation, damages, or monetary loss due to the information herein, either directly or indirectly. By continuing with this book, readers agree that the author is under no circumstances responsible for any losses, indirect or direct, that are incurred as a result of the information presented in this document, including, but not limited to inaccuracies, omissions, and errors. Respective authors own all copyrights not held by the publisher. The information herein is offered for informational purposes solely and is universal as so. The presentation of the information is without contract or any type of guaranteed assurance. Readers acknowledge that the author is not engaging in the rendering of legal, financial, medical, or professional advice. Please consult a licensed professional before attempting any techniques outlined in this book.

TABLE OF CONTENTS

Table of Contents 2
INTRODUCTION 6
Types, Causes and Symptoms 7
    Thrush (Oropharyngeal Candidiasis) 10
    Genital Yeast Infection (Genital Candidiasis) 11
    Diaper Rash from Yeast Infection 12
    Cutaneous Candidiasis 13
    Invasive Candidiasis 13
CANDIDA DIET 15
    Sugar 16
    Fruit and Vegetable 17
    Vitamins and Minerals 19
    Fat 20
    Probiotics and Dairy Products 20
    Protein 22
Tips and Tricks 25
BREAKFAST RECIPES 28
    Hazelnuts Pancakes 29
    Baby Kale Omelette 31
    Eggplant Waffles 33
    Rutabaga Pancakes 35

- Hemp Seed Porridge ... 37
- Sorghum Breakfast Pudding ... 39
- Parsnips Barley Muffins ... 41
- Beet Greens Asparagus Quiche Cups ... 43
- Chickpeas Flour Pancakes ... 45
- Quinoa & Flax Porridge ... 47

LUNCH RECIPES ... 49
- Sardines Salad ... 50
- Cranberry Beans & Pork Chili ... 52
- Turkey & Flax Seeds Salad ... 54
- Peach Chutney Lamb Curry ... 56
- Scallops & Avocado Salad ... 58
- Grilled Beef with Pesto ... 60
- One-Pot Pork & Pepper Stew ... 62
- Garlicky Lime Halibut ... 64
- Jerk Lamb ... 66
- Zucchini Lasagna ... 68

DINNER RECIPES ... 70
- Raisins Cider Pork ... 71
- Black Beans, Kale, and Barley Patties ... 73
- Hemp & Basil Scallops ... 75
- Peaches & Carrot Teff ... 77
- Pine Nuts Baked Mackerel ... 79

Basil Orange Mackerel Bowls 81

Northern Beans Soup 83

Balsamic Vinegar Glazed Beef 85

Garlic Cilantro Crabmeat 87

Creamy Avocado Orange Trout 89

DESSERT RECIPES 91

Chocolate Barley Pudding 92

Black Beans Chocolate Cake 94

Vanilla Cassava Flour Cupcakes 96

Orange Cupcakes 98

Peach Balls 100

Strawberry Clafoutis 102

Layered Raspberry Hemp Pudding 104

Pears and Sunflower Seed Pancakes 106

Chocolate Macadamia Nuts Cake 108

Blueberry Flaxseed Cake 110

SMOOTHIES RECIPES 112

Fruity Smoothie 113

Smoothie with a Twist 115

Smoothie with Passion Fruit and Sunflower Butter 117

Beet Greens Smoothie 119

Goji Berries Smoothie 121

Raspberries, Chia, and Peanut Butter Smoothie 123

Green Apples & Citrus Smoothie 125

Nectarines Smoothie 127

Matcha Smoothie 129

Pears, Turnips & Red Cabbage Smoothie 131

2-Weeks Meal Plan 133

1st Week 134

2nd Week 135

INTRODUCTION

Candida is a fungus, a form of yeast that lives in our mouth and intestines. Its function in our body is to help with the absorption and digestion of food and usually does little harm. However, it may overgrow and become dangerous. Infections with candida are the most prevalent cause of fungal infections around the globe.

Many types of candida are not harmful. There are some types, though, which can cause illness, called candidiasis. Candidiasis is also known as moniliasis, an infectious illness. Among them is candida albicans, which is also the most significant and widespread candida species.

There are several parts of the body where candidiasis may occur. Candidiasis of the vaginal mucous membranes, for example, is known as vaginitis, and it is most frequent in diabetic or pregnant women. A common fungal infection that affects the mucous membranes of the mouth, on the other hand, is called Thrush. It is generally localized and moderate, but it can spread to cause a broad cutaneous eruption. Thrush is more common in bottle-fed newborns and those towards the end of their lives.

Commercial antifungal medications for candidiasis include polyenes, fluoropyrimidines, echinocandins, and azoles. However, the occurrence of intrinsic and acquired resistance to azole antifungals has been extensively established in various Candida species.

In light of the seriousness of this condition and the increasing number of cases, the following sections of this book will examine the symptoms of candidiasis, as well as the causes, diagnosis, complications, and available treatments. But most importantly, this book will present you with delicious and healthy recipes that will relieve your symptoms, help you control your candida, or help you avoid candidiasis entirely.

TYPES, CAUSES AND SYMPTOMS

Candida species come in a number of varieties. More than 90% of infections are caused by five species: Candida glabrata, Candida albicans, Candida parapsilosis, Candida krusei, and Candida tropicalis.

Candida infection manifests itself in a number of ways, with symptoms ranging from moderate to quite aggravating in nature. The signs and symptoms might differ from one individual to the next. Symptoms in the same individual may manifest themselves as, for example, muscular pains one day and stomach issues the next. It is therefore hard for many patients to identify the real cause of their problems.

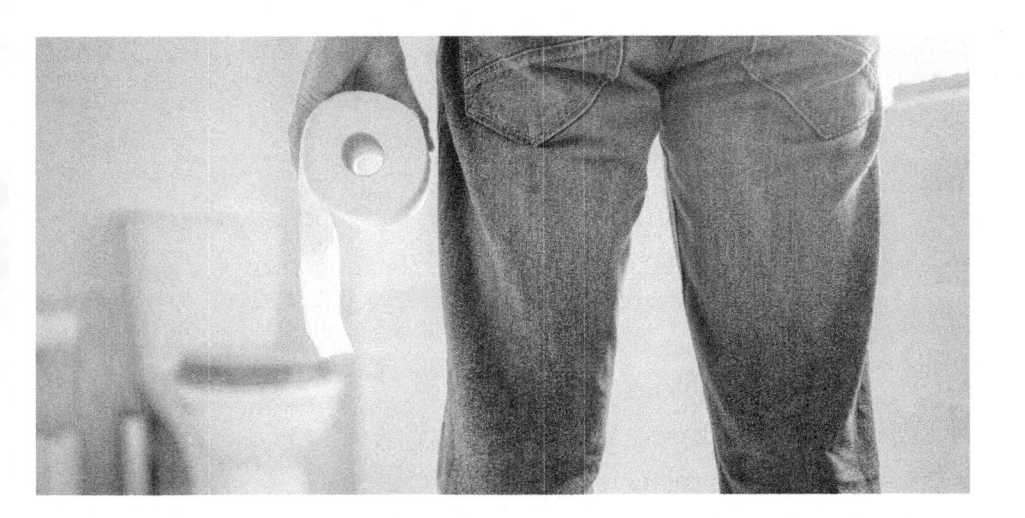

Here are the most common signs and symptoms what you might be suffering from candida overgrowth:

- Fatigue

- Feeling unwell and general malaise
- Mood swings, irritability
- Flatulence
- Diarrhea
- Constipation
- Cramps
- Other digestive problems
- Increased white flow
- Fungus on the fingers
- Fungus in the mouth
- Heavily coated tongue
- Water stagnation
- Swelling
- Itchy skin
- Dermatitis and acne
- Psoriasis
- Allergies
- Inflammation
- Joint pain
- Muscle aches and headaches
- Chronic diseases
- Hormone problems
- Thyroid problems
- Weight loss problems
- Weak immune system
- Anxiety
- Depression

Most candida infections are easily treatable with over-the-counter or prescription drugs and aren't dangerous for your overall health; however, there are candida infections that affect your heart, brain and other internal organs and may be life-threatening. Some of the serious conditions caused by candida also include reflux, rheumatoid diseases, renal and hepatic diseases, psoriasis, cognitive impairment and other serious conditions.

Candida overgrowth may be induced by long-term antibiotic usage, which destroys helpful bacteria that typically keep candida levels in check. Candida may also develop as a consequence of a hormonal imbalance brought on by birth control drugs, adolescence, pregnancy, or menopause, among other things. A poor diet that is high in sugar and processed foods contributes to the condition as well. Many individuals find that eating a well-balanced diet that is rich in organically cultivated foods helps them combat candida.

According to some data, women are more prone to candida than men, and a significant proportion of children also suffer from it. Genetic influence is also thought to be important, especially if the child's mother is suffering from candida problems.

On the following pages are some of the most common types of conditions and diseases caused by candida.

Thrush (Oropharyngeal Candidiasis)

Candida fungus is found in most people's mouths, digestive tracts, and on their skin. Other bacteria and germs in the body generally keep them under control. When sickness, stress, or drugs disrupt this equilibrium, the fungus overgrowths and may produce one of the most common fungal diseases, called Thrush.

Thrush is caused by an overgrowth of Candida albicans. Some people refer to it as oral candidiasis since it spreads into a person's mouth and can also spread to other parts of the body. Thrush infects the cells inside of the mouth. It frequently starts with creamy white patches or blisters on the tongue or surrounding tissues of the mouth. The appearance of thrust in your mouth may look like cottage cheese. A person with Thrush can feel soreness in the tongue and cheeks, as well as may be victims of inflammation and severe pain and redness in the mouth. Thrush can make you feel uncomfortable, but you should not worry about it too much: it may be cured with antifungal medication within a few weeks.

Thrush isn't extremely infectious in most situations, although it may be transferred. Thrush is contagious mostly to individuals who are vulnerable, such as those who have compromised immune systems or are taking certain drugs or medications. If you wish to avoid catching it from another person, avoid coming into touch with their saliva (spit), including kissing, drinking from the same glass, or eating with the same spoon or fork. In addition, always maintain good personal hygiene, such as washing your face and hands regularly, since candida may also be transmitted by hands if the infected person was touching his face or mouth prior to a handshake.

People who are undergoing cancer treatment utilize drugs such as corticosteroids and broad-spectrum antibiotics, as well as people who suffer from diabetes, HIV infections, preached mouth, or are wearing dentures, which are not fitted properly are more prone to develop Trush. In addition, pregnant women and smokers are more likely to suffer from Trush.

Genital Yeast Infection (Genital Candidiasis)

Having a genital yeast infection caused by candida overgrowth is very common among women. Three out of four women may suffer from such infection at least once in their lifetime.

If a woman is suffering from a vaginal fungal infection, she will have a thick white or yellow vaginal secretion, also known as leukorrhea. Another symptom that can be seen is irritation and itching in the genital area.

Vaginal yeast disease can be efficiently treated with medications. If a person has four or more yeast infections in the period of one year, you may require a lengthier treatment period as well as a maintenance plan.

Women who take antibiotics may have an imbalance in their normal vaginal flora as a result, making them more susceptible to developing a yeast infection. In addition, persons with diabetes or a weaker immune system are at a higher risk of developing the condition than others.

Diaper Rash from Yeast Infection

If your baby's diaper is kept damp for a long period of time, your baby might get diaper rashes. These diaper rashes may lead to yeast infection.

It is necessary to inspect your baby's bottom to see if it is red and sensitive, as well as whether there is a raised red border around the sores, in the event that the diaper rush continues. You may treat it with an antifungal cream, but when it comes to your child's health, you should always speak with your doctor. Keep the bottom of the infant clean and dry in order to avoid diaper rashes and candidiasis in the future.

Cutaneous Candidiasis

The fungal infection which affects the person's skin is called Cutaneous candidiasis. In this case, people usually have lesions on the skin which look like red and irritating patches on the skin. These lesions can be of any size and shape. Crusts can develop on the scalp, resulting in hair loss. The infection has the potential to spread to the face, fingers, or limbs.

There is nothing wrong with fungus in or on our bodies. However, if the fungus overgrows, it might create an infection in the surrounding region. Overgrowth is more common in warm, damp environments or where a persistent diaper rash is already present.

Invasive Candidiasis

Candida may grow and expand to the heart, brain, blood, eyes, and bones if it enters the bloodstream. In this case, it may become life-threatening. Invasive candidiasis may occur. This is the most dangerous type of candida infection.

People who are admitted to hospitals or who are living in healthcare institutions such as nursing homes are more likely to get these diseases than the general public. This is due to the fact that such individuals often suffer from a variety of health issues or diseases, as well as a weaker immune system. It is possible that people will be impacted by contamination from tools if they are not properly maintained.

Candida can enter your circulation if your digestive tract lining has been damaged or inflamed, if you have had gastrointestinal surgery or puncture, or if you have had a central venous catheter placed into your arm or hand. Candida may invade your organs through the circulation owing to a compromised immune system caused by therapies such as chemotherapy or corticosteroid therapy.

Antibiotics that are used often or for a long period of time (which target many different kinds of bacteria in the body) depletes your gut flora and impairs your immune system" s ability to fight candida.

Invasive candidiasis may be treated with an antifungal medication, which can be taken orally or intravenously. If you have a high risk of yeast infection and are scheduled for surgery, your doctor may prescribe an antifungal treatment regimen before the procedure.

One of the very rare but severe forms of candida is Candidiasis of Mucosa. This kind of infection is classified as chronic infection of the mucous membrane and may be life-threatening. Other than that, it can infect the skin and nails. This type of illness is common amongst children. It may be identified by red, crusty, and thicker lesions, mainly on the nose and forehead.

CANDIDA DIET

One of the necessary things that may help you get candida under control is a healthy diet. In general, Candida diet or candida cleans is very strict as it eliminates all sources of wheat, sugar, and yeast from your diet while promoting lean proteins, non-starchy vegetables, and healthy fats, as well as various supplements to aid the healing process.

The purpose of this diet is to reestablish a healthy ratio between lactic acid bacteria and yeasts so that candida remains in the body but within the healthy limits. Once we achieve such a result, it is pointless to switch to the old tracks, as candida multiplies quickly again. To avoid that, it makes more sense to talk about a proper, healthy diet that becomes part of lasting care for your health.

Candida diet is not time-limited. Some patients have been suffering from their ailment for years, if not decades, so expecting a quick and easy remedy is generally unrealistic. Some dieters may see long-term remission from candida infections within several weeks. Others may require six months or more and perhaps require a lifelong elimination of white carbohydrates, sugary foods, and alcohol to keep the overgrowth from reoccurring.

For a start, make sure you may not have allergies or intolerances to certain foods. If your body has difficulty breaking down and digesting certain substances, these can accumulate in your gut and feed on candida, which will make the situation significantly worse. Instead of recklessly eliminating wheat products, milk, dairy products and yeast, it makes sense to first make sure what you are really allergic or intolerant to.

Sugar

Candida feeds on sugar. If on the Candida diet, you should give up sucrose and glucose, which can be found in sweets and many pre-prepared meals. In any case, this food is far from good for your health. Sugar is included in all types of sweets, alcohol, many beverages and processed foods, which should be avoided at all costs. It is best to avoid alcoholic beverages as much as possible, as they contain a high percentage of sugar.

Several controversies raise the question of whether the sugar in fruit can also be harmful. Some people tolerate fruit well, while it may cause certain problems with others. Since fruit has many other beneficial effects, especially if it is organically grown, it makes sense to eliminate all other unhealthy sources of sugar from your diet before you start to avoid fruit.

Fruit and Vegetable

When choosing vegetables, have in mind the amount of starch they include. Starch is a type of complex carbohydrate which is contained in all vegetables. Some veggies contain significantly smaller amounts than others, resulting in their lower glycemic index (GI). GI assesses how rapidly carbs boost blood glucose levels and thus grades them on a scale of 0-100. Low GI carbohydrates are digested, absorbed, and metabolized more slowly. This leads to a lower increase in blood glucose levels, which would otherwise encourage fat storage. Stabilized blood sugar levels have been shown in studies to provide a variety of benefits, including sustained weight loss, reduced belly fat, and so on. To keep your blood sugar stabilized and your digestion fast and running, it is advised to eat mainly low GI vegetables.

Vegetables with the lowest GI include spinach, Bok choy, lettuce, green collards, radishes (red and white), mung bean, celery, and arugula. For a moderate carbohydrate intake, you can add to your menu cauliflower, kale, avocado, asparagus, cucumber, olives and cabbage, scallions, okra, eggplant, broccoli, zucchini, tomatoes, and turnips.

As for the fruit, it is filled with vitamins and minerals, which makes it a great snack. However, you are encouraged to eat fruit with a low GI. The same reasons regarding sugar intake, as already explained above, applies. In limited amounts, you may eat sour and less sugary fruit, such as berries (raspberries, blueberries, cranberries), green apples and citrusy fruit, such as oranges, lemons, or grapefruits.

Vitamins and Minerals

It makes sense to test your levels of iron, potassium and other minerals. Like many other fungi, candida is dependent on oxygen deficiency. If your blood does not contain enough iron to carry oxygen around your body, this is good news for candida but much worse for your well-being and health. No strict diet will work if the real culprit for your problems is actually iron deficiency.

It is also advisable to ensure an adequate intake of vitamins and minerals - in the event of an imbalance; your body absorbs the nutrients it needs to function normally. Not only fruit and vegetables - many fresh herbs and spices include a lot of vitamins and minerals; some are also full of antioxidants (such as parsley and ginger) or are known to include anti-inflammatory properties (such as cumin, coriander, garlic, ginger, etc.).

Other great examples include garlic, oregano, basil, turmeric, cayenne and black pepper, cinnamon, caraway seed, anise seed, sage, or thyme. Remember, fresh herbs always taste better than processed or dried and include more vitamins.

Fat

A balanced diet is important in maintaining a healthy and strong immune system. Many people with candida are deficient in essential fatty acids, including omega 3 fatty acids, so it is important that your diet is as rich in them as possible. An excellent source can be organically grown flax seeds, which are soaked in water for some time before consumption.

You may also obtain fat from olives, avocado and nuts. Cold-pressed organically grown oils of plant origin, such as cold press olive oil, are also great healthy fat sources.

Probiotics and Dairy Products

There is no doubt that probiotics represent a very effective treatment for candida overgrowth. Probiotics are healthy bacteria that are found in the food you eat or enter your body with nutritional supplements. You can have up to 2 kilograms of bacteria in your digestive system. These clusters of bacteria are called your microbiome, a type of bacterial fingerprint that is unique to you. If you suffer from candida overgrowth, the balance between good and bad bacteria can be destroyed.

Probiotic products boost microorganism growth and help to restore normal levels of the beneficial bacteria that control candida in your gut. Various studies prove that eating probiotics regularly helps with treating as well as preventing candida altogether.

It is best to focus on the right food sources first, as these also contain other nutrients, but also because the quality of nutritional supplements can vary.

Good sources of probiotics include:

- Kombucha
- Kimchi
- Kefir

- Cucumbers
- Tofu

As for other dairy products, the Candida diet restricts the use of full-fat dairy products, with the exception of probiotic yogurt, ghee, and genuine butter (in moderation as it includes saturated fat).

Dairy foods, such as milk and cheese, tend to have a high concentration of natural sugars (such as lactose) and hence may be challenging to digest. It is generally recommended to avoid any sweet milk or yogurt products, such as ice cream or frozen yogurt. In addition, several types of cheeses also include yeast that naturally grows on its skin.

Protein

Protein sources have been essential components of every dining and are significant to our body as protein maintains our cells, organs, and muscles to function properly and also helps guard our body against infections. It is essential to have a high-calorie, high-protein diet when suffering from candida overgrowth in order to obtain as many nutrients as possible. Choose protein sources that are low in fat and prepared in a way to make your digestion easier and to help your gut heal faster.

You are encouraged to eat lean protein sources such as poultry, lean fish and seafood and other types of lean meat. Stay away from fatty meat cuts, organ meat and heavily processed meat products, such as salami, bacon, etc., as such products usually include sugar. Frying is not an option. Fried food includes higher GI, which helps candida grow and expand. Furthermore, it is not only covered in fat and hard to digest, but it also isn't nutritious since many nutrients are lost during the preparation process.

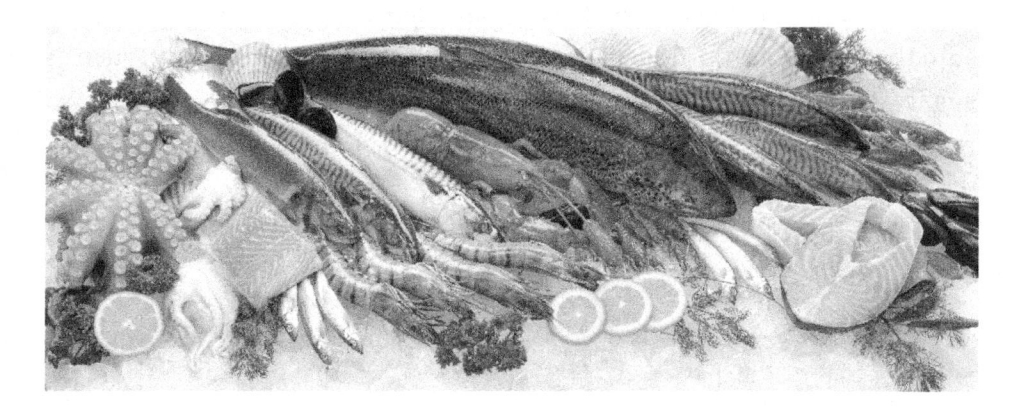

Another great protein source is eggs. Eggs are one of the healthiest and most nutrient-dense foods on the market. However, make sure to cook your eggs thoroughly, as fresh eggs can cause a variety of digestive issues, may include dangerous bacteria and may worsen your illness. Avoid frying and over-seasoning.

In addition, you can eat vegan protein, such as tofu and soy protein, as they include very little fat and are lactose and sugar-free. Similarly, you can grab a vegan dairy source, such as vegan yogurt or sour cream. Just make sure that the chosen products do not include unwanted additives, such as sugar.

TIPS AND TRICKS

Candida infection may be cured and recurrence of its infection avoided most effectively by dealing with the underlying cause of the infection. The kind of food you eat has a considerable influence on the balance of "good" and "bad" microorganisms in your digestive system.

Sugars, carbohydrates, and dairy products may encourage the development of candida and other "bad" microorganisms in the body. It is possible that consuming too many of these foods can increase the development of the sickness if you already have a damaged immune system.

Certain foods, on the other hand, have been shown to specifically boost the development of "good" bacteria while inhibiting the growth of candida, which may have a variety of effects on a person's body depending on the situation.

If you are in good health, you may get infected with Candida albicans fairly regularly, and you may not need treatment. However, if your immune system is somewhat compromised or you are suffering from other illnesses, such as diabetes, or under a lot of stress and sleep-deprived, your candida levels may rise and cause you much trouble.

To sum up, when candida spreads too much, exclude from the diet:

- all types of sugar, including corn and maple syrup and molasses, including sweets;
- processed and pre-prepared food, which include sugar or wheat;
- fruit and vegetables with a high GI;
- yeast and foods containing it, including wheat and products made out of wheat;

- vinegar (except apple cider vinegar, since it may make your body less hospitable to fungus due to its PH level balancing properties);
- mushrooms, as they are a type of fungus;
- alcohol and caffeine;
- saturated fats;
- animal dairy (milk, cheese, cottage cheese) or products containing lactose.

Refrain from excessive use of birth control pills and antibiotics unless absolutely necessary. Try to find other healthy alternatives. If you need to take antibiotics, be sure to get probiotics as well. This will help keep the healthy bacteria present in your body.

Dealing with candida can be quite exhausting, mainly due to the fact that it is usually very difficult to figure out what is wrong at all. In many people, the symptoms become so severe that they even need a sick leave. However, as with other health problems, it is recommended that you be as physically active as possible with candida. Exercise increases the level of oxygen in your body, which is very useful in fighting candida spores, and at the same time, reduces stress levels.

The best strategy to avoid candida overgrowth is to practice good hygiene and consume nutritious foods. Thrush in the mouth can be avoided by practicing proper oral hygiene. Maintaining body hygiene can help in reducing the risk of Genital candidiasis. A balanced diet can help you avoid many issues and boost your immune system.

On the following pages, you can find many healthy and easy-to-make recipes tailored for the Candida diet to help you get your Candida levels under control. At the end of the book, there is a 2-week diet plan to help you transition to your diet. So, let's not waste any more time. Grab your apron and let's head into the kitchen!

BREAKFAST RECIPES

Hazelnuts Pancakes

| Prep time: 15 min | Cook time: 30 min | Servings: 2 |

Ingredients

- *1 avocado*
- *2 tbsp stevia*
- *6 large eggs, separated*
- *4 tbsp melted butter, plus more for serving*
- *½ cup hazelnuts flour*
- *1/2 tsp baking soda*
- *pinch of kosher salt*
- *cooking spray*

Directions

- Whisk together avocado, egg yolks, stevia, and melted butter in a large mixing dish. Fold in the hazelnuts flour, baking soda, and salt until barely mixed.
- Whip egg whites in a separate large mixing basin with a hand or stand mixer until stiff peaks form, about 4 to 5 minutes. Gently fold in the whipped egg whites until they are uniformly distributed throughout the batter.
- Place a large nonstick pan over medium-low heat and coat it with cooking spray. Pour roughly 2 tablespoons of pancake batter into the pan and evenly spread it out. Flip the pancake when a lip forms around the edge and small bubbles appear (about 1-2 minutes). Cook for a few minutes on each side or until both sides are gently browned.

NUTRITION FACTS (PER SERVING)

Calories	741	
Total Fat	43.6g	56%
Saturated Fat	22.7g	113%
Cholesterol	626mg	209%
Sodium	1195mg	52%
Total Carbohydrate	57.7g	21%
Dietary Fiber	16g	57%
Total Sugars	27.3g	
Protein	32.1g	

Baby Kale Omelette

Prep time: 5 min   Cook time: 10 min   Servings: 2

Ingredients

- *4 eggs*
- *2 cups torn baby kale leaves*
- *1 ½ tablespoons flaxseed*
- *½ teaspoon onion flakes*
- *¼ teaspoon ground cinnamon*
- *salt and pepper to taste*

Directions

- In a mixing dish, whisk together the eggs, then add the baby kale and flaxseed.
- Add onion flakes, cinnamon, salt, and pepper to taste.
- Cook the egg mixture in a small skillet, covered, over medium heat for about 3 minutes, or until partially set.
- Cook for another 2 to 3 minutes after flipping the omelette with a spatula. Reduce heat to low and cook for another 2 to 3 minutes, or until the desired doneness is reached.

NUTRITION FACTS (PER SERVING)

Calories	223	
Total Fat	14.8g	19%
Saturated Fat	6.7g	34%
Cholesterol	347mg	116%
Sodium	409mg	18%
Total Carbohydrate	3.2g	1%
Dietary Fiber	1.1g	4%
Total Sugars	0.9g	
Protein	21.1g	

Eggplant Waffles

Prep time: 15 min | Cook time: 5 min | Servings: 4

Ingredients

- *1-1/2 cups shredded eggplant*
- *1 egg*
- *½ tablespoon sesame oil*
- *1/4 teaspoon onion flacks*
- *1 pinch salt*
- *½ cup flaxseed flour*
- *¼ teaspoon baking powder*

Directions

- Preheat waffle iron as directed by the manufacturer.
- In a mixing dish, combine the eggplant, eggs, sesame oil, onion flacks, and salt. Mix in the flaxseed flour and baking powder until everything is well mixed.
- Pour 1/2 cup of batter into the waffle iron's center. Close the lid and cook for 5 minutes, or until the iron stops steaming and the waffle is crisp.

NUTRITION FACTS (PER SERVING)

Calories	49	
Total Fat	2.9g	4%
Saturated Fat	0.7g	4%
Cholesterol	41mg	14%
Sodium	42mg	2%
Total Carbohydrate	4.1g	1%
Dietary Fiber	0.7g	2%
Total Sugars	0.9g	
Protein	2.2g	

Rutabaga Pancakes

Prep time: 10 min | Cook time: 15 min | Servings: 4

Ingredients

- 2 cups grated peeled rutabaga
- 4 small eggs
- ½ cup finely chopped onion
- 2 tablespoon flaxseed oil
- ½ teaspoon salt
- ½ teaspoon dried thyme
- 1 pinch ground black pepper to taste
- Oil, for frying pan

Directions

- In a mixing bowl, whisk together the rutabaga, eggs, onion, flaxseed oil, salt, thyme, and black pepper until a lumpy batter forms.
- Put a greased, heavy frying pan over medium heat. Pour the batter into the pan and fry until the edges of the pancakes are brown and crispy, about 6 to 7 minutes per side.

NUTRITION FACTS (PER SERVING)

Calories	170	
Total Fat	10.9g	14%
Saturated Fat	2.2g	11%
Cholesterol	138mg	46%
Sodium	641mg	28%
Total Carbohydrate	13.8g	5%
Dietary Fiber	3.7g	13%
Total Sugars	4.1g	
Protein	5.6g	

Hemp Seed Porridge

Prep time: 15 min   Cook time: 0 min   Servings: 2

Ingredients

- ¼ cup hemp seeds
- 1 banana
- 2 dried figs (unsweetened)
- 1 cup (unsweetened) coconut milk
- ¼ teaspoon ground nutmeg
- salt to taste
- ¼ cup fresh berries, or more to taste

Directions

- In a bowl, add the hemp seeds.
- In a blender, combine the banana and figs, then add the coconut milk, nutmeg, and salt. Blend until smooth, then pour over hemp seeds and stir thoroughly. Allow at least 15 minutes for the mixture to thicken.
- Toss the hemp 'porridge' with berries (if desired) and serve.

NUTRITION FACTS (PER SERVING)

Calories	464	
Total Fat	31.3g	40%
Saturated Fat	25.7g	129%
Cholesterol	0mg	0%
Sodium	176mg	8%
Total Carbohydrate	49.5g	18%
Dietary Fiber	9.8g	35%
Total Sugars	29g	
Protein	5.6g	

Sorghum Breakfast Pudding

| Prep time: 5 min | Cook time: 35 min | Servings: 4 |

Ingredients

- *1 cup sorghum*
- *2 cups water*
- *2 cups white grape juice*
- *1 cup chopped nuts of choice (such as almonds, hazelnuts, etc.)*
- *2 tablespoons lime juice*
- *1 teaspoon ground nutmeg, or to taste*
- *salt to taste*
- *2 teaspoons vanilla extract*

Directions

- Rinse the sorghum thoroughly in a colander.
- Allow to drain, then combine sorghum and water in a medium saucepan.
- Over high heat, bring to a boil. Cover the, reduce the heat to low and allow to simmer for 15 minutes or until all water has been absorbed and sorghum is soft.
- Combine the grape juice, nuts, lime juice, nutmeg, and salt in a mixing bowl.
- Cover and continue to cook for another 15 minutes. Add the vanilla extract and mix well. Serve warm.

NUTRITION FACTS (PER SERVING)

Calories	220	
Total Fat	2g	3%
Saturated Fat	0.3g	1%
Cholesterol	0mg	0%
Sodium	38mg	2%
Total Carbohydrate	46.9g	17%
Dietary Fiber	3.1g	11%
Total Sugars	22.6g	
Protein	4.9g	

Parsnips Barley Muffins

Prep time: 20 min | Cook time: 20 min | Pieces: 12

Ingredients

- ½ cup parsnips, grated
- 1 ½ cups stevia
- 1 ¼ cups barley flour
- 5 tablespoons coconut flour
- 1 teaspoon baking powder
- 1 teaspoon ground nutmeg
- ½ cup mashed banana
- ½ cup unsweetened coconut milk
- ¼ cup sesame oil
- 2 eggs
- ¼ teaspoon vanilla extract
- 6 tablespoons chopped raw hazelnuts

Directions

- Preheat oven to 355°F. Line a 12-cup muffin tray with paper liners.
- In a bowl, combine the parsnips and stevia and put aside to allow the parsnips to release the moisture and soften.
- In a large mixing basin, combine barley flour, coconut flour, baking powder, and nutmeg. In a separate bowl, whisk together banana, milk, oil, eggs, and vanilla extract. Combine the wet and dry ingredients in a mixing bowl and stir until just incorporated. Add the parsnips and stevia to the mix.
- Place a quarter cup of batter in each muffin cup and top with chopped almonds. Bake, 20 to 23 minutes until the tops are lightly browned and a toothpick inserted in the center of each muffin comes out clean. Turn off the oven and let the muffins chill inside for 5 minutes without opening the door.

NUTRITION FACTS (PER SERVING)

Calories	112	
Total Fat	7.9g	10%
Saturated Fat	1.4g	7%
Cholesterol	26mg	9%
Sodium	18mg	1%
Total Carbohydrate	5.4g	2%
Dietary Fiber	1.4g	5%
Total Sugars	2.2g	
Protein	2.8g	

Beet Greens Asparagus Quiche Cups

Prep time: 10 min | Cook time: 20 min | Servings: 12

Ingredients

- *1 cup asparagus, chopped*
- *1 package beet greens, chopped*
- *4 eggs, whisked*
- *2/3 cup unsweetened coconut milk*
- *1/2 cup chopped white onion*
- *2 cloves garlic, minced*

- *1 tablespoon cashews paste*
- *1/4 teaspoon salt*
- *1/4 teaspoon pepper*

Directions

- Preheat the oven to 350°F. Spray 12 baking cups liberally with cooking spray or line them with paper liners before baking.
- In a large mixing bowl, combine all ingredients and stir until well blended.
- Fill each of the 12 prepared baking cups nearly to the top with the mixture.
- Bake for 20 minutes, or until the eggs have set and a toothpick inserted in the center comes out clean. Serve right away.

NUTRITION FACTS (PER SERVING)

Calories	202	
Total Fat	10.5g	13%
Saturated Fat	4.2g	21%
Cholesterol	92mg	31%
Sodium	156mg	7%
Total Carbohydrate	23g	8%
Dietary Fiber	6.3g	22%
Total Sugars	11.3g	
Protein	6.1g	

Chickpeas Flour Pancakes

| Prep time: 10 min | Cook time: 10 min | Pieces: 10 |

Ingredients

- *1 ½ cups chickpeas flour*
- *1 tablespoon baking powder*
- *1 teaspoon salt*
- *1 ¾ cups coconut milk*
- *2 eggs*
- *2 tablespoons sesame oil*

Directions

- Sift the chickpeas flour, baking powder, and salt into a large mixing basin.
- Mix in the milk, eggs, and melted butter until no visible lumps remain. Allow 5 minutes for the mixture to rest.
- Melt some butter or oil in a big griddle over medium heat. Pour in enough batter to cover the pan, bake for about two minutes, then flip and fry for a further minute on the other side, after it begins to bubble. Repeat the process until all batter is used.
- Serve the pancakes filled with a salty filling of your choice.

NUTRITION FACTS (PER SERVING)

Calories	308	
Total Fat	10.7g	14%
Saturated Fat	2.1g	10%
Cholesterol	0mg	0%
Sodium	86mg	4%
Total Carbohydrate	47.5g	17%
Dietary Fiber	5g	18%
Total Sugars	26.1g	
Protein	8.6g	

Quinoa & Flax Porridge

| Prep time: 15 min | Cook time: 0 min | Servings: 4 |

Ingredients

- 2 cups quinoa
- ½ cup flaxseed
- 2 cups almond milk
- ½ cup unsweetened coconut yogurt
- ¼ cup flaked hazelnuts, toasted
- 2 oranges, segmented and chopped

Directions

- Add quinoa and flaxseeds to a bowl, and soak overnight in 4 cups of water.
- In a dry frying pan over medium heat, toast the flaked hazelnuts until golden brown on both sides, about 2-3 minutes. Place in an airtight jar and set aside.
- Add all the ingredients, except for hazelnuts, to the quinoa and flaxseed mixture and stir to combine.
- Divide the content between serving bowls and sprinkle with hazelnuts. Serve and enjoy.

NUTRITION FACTS (PER SERVING)

Calories	221	
Total Fat	11.3g	14%
Saturated Fat	7.5g	37%
Cholesterol	39mg	13%
Sodium	219mg	10%
Total Carbohydrate	22.8g	8%
Dietary Fiber	3g	11%
Total Sugars	2.8g	
Protein	7.2g	

LUNCH RECIPES

Sardines Salad

| Prep time: 20 min | Cook time: 0 min | Servings: 2 |

Ingredients

- 1 jalapeno, finely diced
- 1 small onion, minced
- 1 cup chopped zucchini
- 2 5-ounce cans of sardines
- 3 tablespoons chopped green olives
- 1 tablespoon apple cider vinegar
- 1 tablespoon coconut oil
- 1 tablespoon spicy brown mustard
- ¼ teaspoon kosher salt

Directions

- Drain the sardines, add to a bowl and mash lightly with a fork.
- Stir in the chopped vegetables, oil, vinegar, mustard and salt.
- Taste and season with extra salt if necessary. Serve with a slice of yeast-free bread.
- Refrigerate for up to 3 days.

NUTRITION FACTS (PER SERVING)

Calories	408	
Total Fat	26.6g	34%
Saturated Fat	4.5g	23%
Cholesterol	60mg	20%
Sodium	1345mg	58%
Total Carbohydrate	8.7g	3%
Dietary Fiber	1.9g	7%
Total Sugars	4.1g	
Protein	37.8g	

Cranberry Beans & Pork Chili

Prep time: 20 min Cook time: 8 h Servings: 6

Ingredients

- *1-pound lean ground pork*
- *1 large onion, chopped*
- *3 garlic cloves, minced*
- *2 cups diced tomatoes*
- *2 cups cranberry beans, rinsed and drained*
- *2 cups Anasazi beans, rinsed and drained*
- *2 to 3 tablespoons chili powder*
- *2 teaspoons ground cumin*
- *1/2 teaspoon salt*

Directions

- Cook pork, onion, and garlic in a large skillet over medium heat for 6-8 minutes, or until no longer pink, breaking into crumbles. Drain excess liquid.
- Fill a 5-quart slow cooker halfway with the pork mixture. Cover with 1 cup tomatoes, then add all other ingredients.
- Cook on low for 6-8 hours, covered, to enable flavors to meld.
- To obtain the desired consistency, mash the beans. As desired, garnish with toppings, such as freshly chopped herbs or vegetables.

NUTRITION FACTS (PER SERVING)

Calories	607	
Total Fat	7g	9%
Saturated Fat	2.3g	11%
Cholesterol	68mg	23%
Sodium	282mg	12%
Total Carbohydrate	85.1g	31%
Dietary Fiber	21.3g	76%
Total Sugars	4g	
Protein	51.5g	

Turkey & Flax Seeds Salad

Prep time: 30 min   Cook time: 15 min   Servings: 4

Ingredients

- *3 tablespoons lemon juice*
- *1/4 teaspoon pepper*
- *3/4-pound boneless skinless turkey breasts, cut into thin strips*
- *1 tablespoon sesame oil*
- *1/2 cup apple cider vinegar*
- *1/3 cup stevia*
- *1 teaspoon dried minced onion*
- *1 teaspoon ground mustard*
- *1/2 teaspoon salt*
- *1 cup canola oil*
- *1 tablespoon flax seeds*

For the Salad

- *1 package (6 ounces) fresh baby kale*
- *2 cups sliced fresh raspberries*
- *1 cup fresh fava beans, trimmed*
- *1 small red onion, chopped*
- *1/2 cup walnuts halves, toasted*

Directions

- Combine the lemon juice, pepper, and turkey in a large mixing basin. Refrigerate for 2 hours after covering. Drain and toss out the marinade. Sauté the turkey in oil, on all sides, in a large skillet until it is no longer pink, about 5 minutes.
- Meanwhile, combine the vinegar, stevia, onion, mustard, and salt in a blender. Add flaxseeds and canola oil in a steady stream while the processor is running.
- Add all the salad ingredients to the bowl, add the turkey and pour over the dressing. Serve immediately.

NUTRITION FACTS (PER SERVING)

Calories	324	
Total Fat	11.6g	15%
Saturated Fat	2.2g	11%
Cholesterol	76mg	25%
Sodium	423mg	18%
Total Carbohydrate	27.2g	10%
Dietary Fiber	3.8g	14%
Total Sugars	21.7g	
Protein	28.2g	

Peach Chutney Lamb Curry

Prep time: 10 min   Cook time: 10 min   Servings: 4

Ingredients

- *1 tablespoon sesame oil*
- *1-pound boneless skinless lamb, cubed*
- *1 tablespoon curry powder*
- *2 garlic cloves, minced*
- *1/4 teaspoon salt*
- *1/4 teaspoon pepper*
- *1 cup water*
- *1/2 cup peach chutney, unsweetened*
- *1/2 cup coconut cream, unsweetened*

Directions

- Brown the lamb in a large skillet over medium-high heat, greased with sesame oil.
- Cook for an additional 1-2 minutes, stirring in the curry powder, garlic, salt, and pepper.
- Cover with water and bring to a boil. Add more water if necessary to cover the meat.
- Reduce heat to low and cook, uncovered, for 10 minutes, or until the meat is well done, stirring periodically. Remove from the heat.
- Combine the chutney and cream in a mixing bowl. Add gradually to the cooked lamb, stirring to combine.

NUTRITION FACTS (PER SERVING)

Calories	343	
Total Fat	15.6g	20%
Saturated Fat	4.8g	24%
Cholesterol	112mg	37%
Sodium	328mg	14%
Total Carbohydrate	16.8g	6%
Dietary Fiber	0.6g	2%
Total Sugars	12.1g	
Protein	34g	

Scallops & Avocado Salad

Prep time: 10 min   Cook time: 15 min   Servings: 4

Ingredients

- *1-pound uncooked scallops*
- *1 small garlic clove, minced*
- *1/2 teaspoon chili powder*
- *1/4 teaspoon salt*
- *1/4 teaspoon ground cumin*
- *2 teaspoons olive oil*
- *5 cups lettuces*
- *1 cup frozen fava beans, thawed*
- *1 cup jicama*
- *1/2 cup chopped sweet red pepper*
- *1 medium ripe avocado, peeled and thinly sliced*

Basil Vinaigrette

- *7 tablespoons canola oil*

- *1/4 cup minced fresh basil*
- *1/4 cup lemon juice*
- *1-1/2 teaspoons stevia*
- *1 small garlic clove, minced*
- *1/2 teaspoon salt*
- *1/4 teaspoon pepper*

Directions

- Cook the scallops, garlic, chili powder, salt, and cumin in oil, in a large skillet, over medium heat for 3-4 minutes, or until pink; set aside.
- Combine the lettuces, fava beans, jicama, and red pepper in a large mixing basin. Distribute among 4 serving plates. Serve with scallops and avocado on the top. Whisk together the vinaigrette ingredients in a small dish; drizzle over the salad.

NUTRITION FACTS (PER SERVING)

Calories	290	
Total Fat	12.8g	16%
Saturated Fat	2.5g	13%
Cholesterol	162mg	54%
Sodium	331mg	14%
Total Carbohydrate	22g	8%
Dietary Fiber	7g	25%
Total Sugars	5.2g	
Protein	25.8g	

Grilled Beef with Pesto

Prep time: 25 min | Cook time: 10 min | Servings: 6

Ingredients

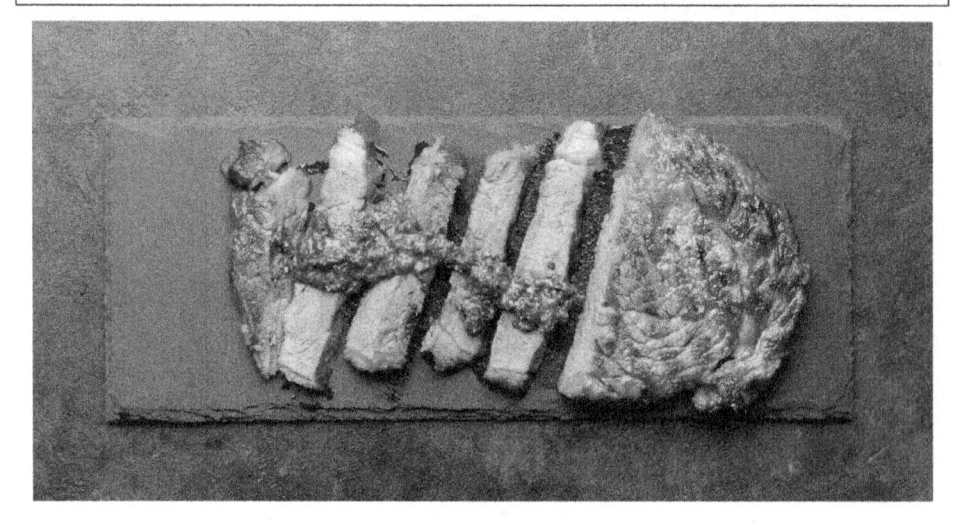

- 1/2 cup chopped onion
- 1/2 cup lemon juice
- 1/4 cup finely chopped and seeded bell peppers
- 2 tablespoons olive oil
- 4 teaspoons ground cumin
- 1-1/2 pounds beef tenderloin, cut into 3/4-inch slices
- 2 medium ripe avocados, peeled and chopped
- 1 small cucumber, seeded and chopped
- 2 plum tomatoes, seeded and chopped
- 2 green onions, chopped
- 2 tablespoons fresh, homemade pesto

Directions

- To make the marinade, combine the first five ingredients.
- Toss the meat with 1/2 cup of marinade in a large mixing bowl; refrigerate for up to 2 hours, covered.
- Drain the beef and discard the marinade.
- In a small saucepan, add the remaining marinade; bring to a boil. Cook and whisk for 1-2 minutes, or until slightly thickened; remove from heat.
- In a large mixing basin, combine the avocados, cucumber, tomatoes, onions and pesto. Stir well to combine after adding the remaining marinade.
- Place the beef on a grill rack that has been lightly greased over medium heat. Grill for 4-5 minutes per side, covered, until a thermometer reads 145°, brushing with glaze during the last 3 minutes. Serve with a side of pesto.

NUTRITION FACTS (PER SERVING)

Calories	332	
Total Fat	22g	28%
Saturated Fat	5.6g	28%
Cholesterol	70mg	23%
Sodium	62mg	3%
Total Carbohydrate	10.8g	4%
Dietary Fiber	4.7g	17%
Total Sugars	3.9g	
Protein	24.3g	

One-Pot Pork & Pepper Stew

| Prep time: 10 min | Cook time: 30 min | Servings: 4 |

Ingredients

- *1-pound lean ground pork*
- *3 cups diced tomatoes, undrained*
- *4 large Jalapenos, coarsely chopped*
- *1 large onion, chopped*
- *2 green chiles, chopped*
- *3 teaspoons garlic, minced*
- *1 teaspoon pepper*
- *1/4 teaspoon salt*
- *2 cups water*
- *2 cups quinoa*

Directions

- Cook pork in a 6-quart stockpot over medium heat until no longer pink, about 6-8 minutes.
- Add the tomatoes, jalapenos, onion, chiles, and seasonings.
- Bring to a boil after adding water, then reduce to low heat and cook, covered, for 20-25 minutes, or until veggies are soft.
- Follow the package directions for cooking quinoa.
- Add quinoa to the stew a few minutes prior to the end of cooking, stir to combine.

NUTRITION FACTS (PER SERVING)		
Calories	311	
Total Fat	4.1g	5%
Saturated Fat	1.5g	7%
Cholesterol	51mg	17%
Sodium	149mg	6%
Total Carbohydrate	45.3g	16%
Dietary Fiber	3g	11%
Total Sugars	4.2g	
Protein	21.9g	

Garlicky Lime Halibut

| Prep time: 10 min | Cook time: 30 min | Servings: 4 |

Ingredients

- *3 tbsp almond butter, divided*
- *2 tbsp sesame oil, divided*
- *1 lb. green beans*
- *4 (4-oz.) halibut fillets*
- *Sea salt*
- *Black pepper*
- *3 cloves garlic, minced*
- *1/4 tsp crushed red pepper flakes*
- *1 lime, sliced*
- *Zest and juice of 1 lime*
- *1 tbsp freshly chopped cilantro, plus more for garnish*

Directions

- Melt 1 tbsp almond butter and 2 tbsp sesame oil in a large skillet over medium heat.
- Season the halibut with salt and pepper. 4 to 5 minutes per side until golden. Place on a plate to cool.
- Add halibut fillets and green beans and cook for 2 to 4 minutes, or until tender. Transfer to a platter and season with salt and pepper.
- Add the remaining almond butter to the skillet. After the butter has melted, add the garlic and red pepper flakes and simmer for 1 minute, or until aromatic, then add the lime, lime zest, juice, and cilantro. Remove the skillet from the heat, then add the halibut fillets and green beans and spoon over the sauce.
- Before serving, top with additional cilantro.

NUTRITION FACTS (PER SERVING)

Calories	291	
Total Fat	11.1g	14%
Saturated Fat	1.5g	7%
Cholesterol	0mg	0%
Sodium	264mg	11%
Total Carbohydrate	40.4g	15%
Dietary Fiber	6.1g	22%
Total Sugars	2.1g	
Protein	8.5g	

Jerk Lamb

| Prep time: 2 h | Cook time: 20 min | Servings: 2 |

Ingredients

- *1 bunch chives, plus more (thinly sliced) for garnish*
- *2 cloves garlic*
- *1 serrano pepper, roughly chopped*
- *juice of 1 lemon*
- *2 tbsp sesame oil*
- *1 tbsp stevia*
- *1/2 tsp ground cinnamon*
- *1/2 tsp ground nutmeg*
- *1/2 tsp ground clove*
- *1 tsp dried basil*

- *kosher salt*
- *2 tbsp + ¼ cup of water*
- *8 pieces bone-in lamb drumsticks and thighs*
- *vegetable oil for greasing the grill*

Directions

- In a blender, blend together chives, garlic, serrano pepper, lemon juice, oil, stevia, cinnamon, nutmeg, clove, basil, 1 tsp salt, and 2 tbsp of water, until smooth.
- Place 1/4 cup of water in a separate bowl. Season the lamb with salt and pepper in a shallow dish.
- Pour the marinade over the lamb and toss to coat. Allow marinating in the fridge for at least 2 hours or up to overnight, turning once or twice. Set aside some marinade for later.
- Preheat the grill to medium-high and oil the grates when ready to grill. Grill the lamb for about 10 minutes, regularly flipping, until browned in areas. Transfer the lamb to a cooler portion of the grill and brush with the marinade. Cook for 10 to 15 more minutes, covered until the lamb is cooked to your liking.
- Serve with a fresh salad or cooked vegetables.

NUTRITION FACTS (PER SERVING)

Calories	433	
Total Fat	21.2g	27%
Saturated Fat	4.4g	22%
Cholesterol	0mg	0%
Sodium	1267mg	55%
Total Carbohydrate	27.4g	10%
Dietary Fiber	10.3g	37%
Total Sugars	7.5g	
Protein	44.4g	

Zucchini Lasagna

Prep time: 15 min   Cook time: 1 h 40 min   Servings: 4

Ingredients

- 2 medium zucchinis, thinly sliced into 1/4" thick slices
- kosher salt & freshly ground black pepper
- 1 tbsp coconut oil
- 3 cloves garlic, minced
- 1 onion, chopped
- 2 tsp dried basil
- 1/4 c. chopped fresh cilantro, plus more for garnish
- 1 large egg
- 1 25-oz. jar tomatoes

Directions

- Preheat the oven to 400°F.
- Season zucchini sliced with salt and place them on a cooling rack. Allow for a 20-minute rest period. With a paper towel, pat the salted sides. Allow for another 20 minutes after flipping and seasoning. Using a paper towel, pat dry.
- Heat the oil in a large skillet over medium heat. Add the garlic, onions, and basil to the pan. Cook until the onions are transparent. Season with salt and pepper.
- Wisk together the egg, basil and cilantro in a mixing basin, season with salt and pepper to taste.
- Spread a thin layer of tomato sauce, a single layer of zucchini "noodles," and a layer of egg mixture in a 9" x 13" casserole dish; repeat the layers. Finish with tomato sauce and egg mixture on top of the last layer of zucchini. Bake for 35 minutes, covered with foil. Remove the foil if preferred and broil for 1 to 2 minutes, or until brown on top. Allow 10 min to cool before garnishing with parsley and serving.

NUTRITION FACTS (PER SERVING)

Calories	279	
Total Fat	8.8g	11%
Saturated Fat	0.5g	3%
Cholesterol	45mg	15%
Sodium	169mg	7%
Total Carbohydrate	23.8g	9%
Dietary Fiber	2.5g	9%
Total Sugars	18.4g	
Protein	29.5g	

DINNER RECIPES

Raisins Cider Pork

| Prep time: 15 min | Cook time: 45 min | Servings: 6 |

Ingredients

- *1 tbsp sesame oil*
- *1 lb. pork*
- *2 tbsp almond butter*
- *1/2 cup raisins*
- *1/3 cups apple cider vinegar*
- *2 cloves garlic, minced*
- *1 tbsp stevia*
- *Zest of 1 lime*
- *6 sprigs sage*
- *2 tbsp chopped basil and thyme leaves*

Directions

- Preheat the oven to 325°F.
- Heat sesame oil in a large ovenproof skillet over medium-high heat. Cook the pork in oil until the skin is brown and crispy, about 4 minutes, with the skin side down. Remove the pork from the fire and set it skin side up on a plate.
- In the same skillet, melt the almond butter, then add the raisins, vinegar, garlic, stevia, and lime zest. Return the pork to the skillet and scatter the herbs on top. Cook for 5 to 10 minutes, or until the liquid thickens and the raisins soften.
- Put in the oven and cook for another 18 to 25 minutes, or until the pork is cooked through.

NUTRITION FACTS (PER SERVING)

Calories	195	
Total Fat	13.1g	17%
Saturated Fat	4.9g	24%
Cholesterol	70mg	23%
Sodium	79mg	3%
Total Carbohydrate	7.3g	3%
Dietary Fiber	1.7g	6%
Total Sugars	4.7g	
Protein	13.2g	

Black Beans, Kale, and Barley Patties

Prep time: 15 min | Cook time: 40 min | Servings: 4

Ingredients

- 1/4 cups crumbled halloumi cheese
- 1 clove garlic
- 1 serrano chili, seeded
- kosher salt
- 1/2 cups packed baby kale
- 1/2 cups cooked barley
- 1 15-oz can black beans, rinsed
- 1 tbsp olive oil
- 2 spring onions, quartered lengthwise, plus more for serving
- mixed green salad, for serving

Directions

- Preheat the oven to 425°F. Pulse the halloumi cheese, garlic, chili, and 2 tsp salt in a food processor until almost smooth.
- Pulse a couple more times to chop the kale, barley and black beans.
- Using oil, coat a rimmed baking sheet. Scoop the pulsed mixture into 2-tablespoon balls, place them on a baking sheet, and slightly flatten them. Roast for 8 to 9 minutes, or until the bottoms are golden brown. Cook for another 7 to 8 minutes, or until golden brown on the other side.
- Serve with a salad of mixed greens and spring onions.

NUTRITION FACTS (PER SERVING)

Calories	314	
Total Fat	19.5g	25%
Saturated Fat	9.2g	46%
Cholesterol	77mg	26%
Sodium	504mg	22%
Total Carbohydrate	18.4g	7%
Dietary Fiber	6.3g	23%
Total Sugars	4g	
Protein	20.6g	

Hemp & Basil Scallops

| Prep time: 10 min | Cook time: 25 min | Servings: 4 |

Ingredients

- *1 tablespoon hemp seeds*
- *1-pound uncooked scallops peeled and deveined*
- *a sprinkle of salt and pepper*
- *1/4 cup chopped fresh basil*
- *1 tsp lemon zest*
- *lemon wedges*

Directions

- Preheat a large nonstick skillet over medium heat. Add the hemp seeds and toast for about 1 minute.
- Cook and stir for 1 minute after adding the scallops.
- Season with salt and pepper to taste, then stir in the basil and lemon zest and simmer, uncovered, for another 1-2 minutes, or until the scallops turn pink.
- Squeeze the lemon juice over the top and sprinkle with additional fresh basil to serve.

NUTRITION FACTS (PER SERVING)

Calories	305	
Total Fat	11.1g	14%
Saturated Fat	4.6g	23%
Cholesterol	79mg	26%
Sodium	738mg	32%
Total Carbohydrate	16.8g	6%
Dietary Fiber	2g	7%
Total Sugars	4.2g	
Protein	28.5g	

Peaches & Carrot Teff

Prep time: 10 min | Cook time: 15 min | Servings: 6

Ingredients

- 2-1/4 cups vegetable stock
- 1 cup teff, rinsed
- 2 tablespoons sesame oil
- 3 medium carrots, peeled and cut into 1/2-inch pieces
- 2 onions, finely chopped
- 3 medium peaches, cut into 1/4-inch slices
- 1/2 cup vermouth
- 1/2 teaspoon salt
- 1 can (15 ounces) chickpeas, rinsed and drained

Directions

- Bring the stock and teff to a boil in a large saucepan. Reduce the heat to low; cover and cook for 15-20 minutes, or until the liquid is almost completely absorbed. Remove the pan from the heat.
- Meanwhile, heat the oil in a 6-quart stockpot over medium heat. Cook and stir for 5 minutes after adding the carrot and onion. Cook and stir for a further 6-8 minutes after adding the peaches, or until all the ingredients are soft.
- Combine the vermouth and salt in a mixing bowl. Bring to a boil, then reduce to low heat and cook, uncovered, for 1 minute, or until the wine has evaporated.
- Incorporate all the ingredients and stir well to combine.

NUTRITION FACTS (PER SERVING)

Calories	375	
Total Fat	30.1g	39%
Saturated Fat	14.1g	70%
Cholesterol	86mg	29%
Sodium	1070mg	47%
Total Carbohydrate	6.8g	2%
Dietary Fiber	1.9g	7%
Total Sugars	2g	
Protein	20g	

Pine Nuts Baked Mackerel

Prep time: 20 min   Cook time: 15 min   Servings: 6

Ingredients

- 6 mackerel fillets (6 ounces each)
- 1 cup pine nuts, chopped
- ½ tbsp stevia
- 3 tablespoons orange juice
- 1 teaspoon chervil
- 1 teaspoon pepper

Directions

- Preheat the oven to 425°F.
- Place the mackerel in a 13x9-inch baking dish that has been buttered. Toss the remaining ingredients together and ladle over the mackerel.
- Bake 12-15 minutes, uncovered, or until fish flakes readily with a fork.
- Serve with a freshly prepared salad.

NUTRITION FACTS (PER SERVING)

Calories	374	
Total Fat	14.1g	18%
Saturated Fat	1.9g	9%
Cholesterol	91mg	30%
Sodium	537mg	23%
Total Carbohydrate	13.1g	5%
Dietary Fiber	3.7g	13%
Total Sugars	8.9g	
Protein	48.1g	

Basil Orange Mackerel Bowls

Prep time: 15 min | Cook time: 45 min | Servings: 4

Ingredients

- *3 jalapenos, sliced into strips*
- *2/3 cup coconut oil, plus 1 tablespoon*
- *kosher salt and freshly ground black pepper*
- *1/3 cup orange juice*
- *2 tbsp finely chopped basil, plus more for serving*
- *2 tsp stevia*
- *1 garlic clove, minced*
- *4 mackerel fillets*
- *4 cup cooked quinoa*

- *1 avocado, thinly sliced*
- *orange wedges, for serving*

Directions

- Preheat the oven to 400°Ft and lay a large baking sheet with parchment paper. Toss jalapenos with 1 tablespoon coconut oil on a baking sheet. Season with salt and pepper and bake for 10 minutes in the oven.
- Meanwhile, make the basil orange marinade by whisking together the remaining coconut oil, orange juice, basil, stevia, and garlic. Season the fish with salt and pepper in a large mixing basin. Half of the marinade should be poured over the fillets. Toss until everything is evenly coated.
- Lay the fillets on top of the peppers and bake for another 15 to 20 minutes, or until peppers and mackerel are cooked through.
- To make the bowls, divide the quinoa amongst four bowls and top with mackerel, jalapenos, avocado, and a wedge of orange. Serve with additional marinade on the side and garnished with basil.

NUTRITION FACTS (PER SERVING)

Calories	930	
Total Fat	27.7g	35%
Saturated Fat	4.9g	24%
Cholesterol	0mg	0%
Sodium	53mg	2%
Total Carbohydrate	157.3g	57%
Dietary Fiber	10.9g	39%
Total Sugars	5.3g	
Protein	16g	

Northern Beans Soup

| Prep time: 15 min | Cook time: 35 min | Servings: 4 |

Ingredients

- 2 tbsp sesame oil
- 1 medium onion, finely chopped
- 1 bell pepper, minced
- 2 cloves garlic, minced
- 1 tbsp tomato paste
- kosher salt
- freshly ground black pepper
- 1/2 tsp ground cumin
- 1 tsp chili powder
- 3 cups northern beans, drained
- 3 cups water or vegetable broth
- 1 bay leaf

Directions

- Heat the oil in a big pot over medium heat. Cook, stirring occasionally, until the onion is tender and transparent, about 5 minutes. Add bell pepper and garlic and cook for a further 2 min, or until aromatic.
- Cook for another minute after adding the tomato paste and stirring to coat the vegetables. Stir in the salt, pepper, cumin, and chili powder to the pot.
- Add the remaining ingredients to the pot and bring to a boil. Reduce to low heat and cook for 15 to 20 minutes, or until slightly reduced and thickened (if you want a thinner soup, add extra broth as needed.) Remove the bay leaf and set it aside to cool. Blend the soup until it reaches the desired consistency.

NUTRITION FACTS (PER SERVING)

Calories	607	
Total Fat	10.4g	13%
Saturated Fat	1.9g	9%
Cholesterol	0mg	0%
Sodium	631mg	27%
Total Carbohydrate	96.1g	35%
Dietary Fiber	23.3g	83%
Total Sugars	5.5g	
Protein	35.8g	

Balsamic Vinegar Glazed Beef

Prep time: 15 min   Cook time: 35 min   Servings: 6

Ingredients

- *1 large potato, peeled and cubed*
- *2 pears, sliced*
- *2 tbsp sesame oil, divided*
- *1 tbsp chopped fresh thyme*
- *kosher salt & freshly ground black pepper*
- *6 beef tenderloin*
- *2/3 cups balsamic vinegar*
- *2 tbsp stevia*
- *1 tbsp mustard*
- *1 tbsp butter*
- *3 thyme sprigs for skillet*

Directions

- Preheat the oven to 425°Ft. Season potatoes and pears in a medium bowl with thyme, 1 tbsp of oil, salt and pepper. Toss until well blended.
- Heat the remaining sesame oil in a large ovenproof skillet over medium-high heat. Sear the beef, skin side down, until golden brown, about 2 minutes. Remove the beef from the pan and set it aside while you prepare the glaze.
- Combine balsamic vinegar, stevia, and mustard in the same skillet. Bring the mixture to a fast simmer and cook until it has somewhat reduced before whisking in the butter. Return the skin-side up beef to the skillet, and surround it with the potato mixture and thyme sprigs. Remove the skillet from the heat and place it in the oven.
- Bake for 20 minutes, or until the potatoes are soft and the beef is cooked through. Serve with the pan drippings.

NUTRITION FACTS (PER SERVING)

Calories	397	
Total Fat	25.8g	33%
Saturated Fat	8.7g	44%
Cholesterol	103mg	34%
Sodium	135mg	6%
Total Carbohydrate	26g	9%
Dietary Fiber	3.1g	11%
Total Sugars	18.4g	
Protein	17.7g	

Garlic Cilantro Crabmeat

| Prep time: 10 min | Cook time: 20 min | Servings: 4 |

Ingredients

- *4 tbsp coconut oil, divided*
- *3 cloves garlic, minced*
- *2 tsp orange juice*
- *1/2 tsp chili powder*
- *1/4 tsp kosher salt*
- *1/3 c chopped cilantro, plus more for serving*
- *1 lb. crabmeat*
- *1/3 cup finely diced onion*

Directions

- Add 3 tablespoons of coconut oil, garlic, orange juice, chili powder, salt, and cilantro in a small bowl and stir to combine.
- Pour the mixture over the crab meat.
- Toss the crabmeat in the mixture until well covered. Refrigerate for 10 minutes or up to 8 hours, covered.
- Warm the remaining tablespoon of coconut oil in a skillet over medium-high heat. Add the onions and cook for 2 to 3 minutes, or until the onions are aromatic. Add the crab meat and cook for 45 seconds on one side, then flip and cook for another 45 seconds.
- Cook for another minute, if necessary, until the shrimp is fully cooked. If preferred, top with more cilantro right away.

NUTRITION FACTS (PER SERVING)

Calories	484	
Total Fat	30.9g	40%
Saturated Fat	4g	20%
Cholesterol	446mg	149%
Sodium	814mg	35%
Total Carbohydrate	7.4g	3%
Dietary Fiber	1g	4%
Total Sugars	1.7g	
Protein	49.4g	

Creamy Avocado Orange Trout

| Prep time: 10 min | Cook time: 30 min | Servings: 4 |

Ingredients

- 4 trout fillets, skins removed (about 2 lbs. total)
- 2 tbsp olive oil
- 1 tbsp stevia
- 2 cloves garlic, minced
- 1/2 tsp chili powder
- 1/4 tsp kosher salt
- 1/4 tsp freshly ground black pepper
- 1/4 cup flax seeds

For the Sauce

- 1 avocado, diced
- juice of 1 orange
- 2 tbsp fresh basil

- *1 tbsp Greek yogurt*
- *1 tbsp sesame oil*
- *kosher salt*

Directions

- Preheat the oven to 375°F. Line a baking sheet with aluminum foil.
- Once the tout is rinsed, use a paper towel, and pat it dry before placing it on a baking pan. Combine olive oil, stevia, garlic, chili powder, salt, and pepper in a small bowl. Spread 1 tablespoon flax seeds over each fillet after pouring over the prepared mixture. Put in the oven.
- Depending on thickness, bake the fish for 15 to 20 minutes (about 10 minutes per 1" thickness, measured from the thickest part of the fillet). Broil the last 3 minutes for crispier edges.
- Make the sauce in the meantime: in a food processor, combine all sauce ingredients and pulse until smooth. Taste and season with salt as needed.
- Remove the fish from the oven and serve with the sauce.

NUTRITION FACTS (PER SERVING)

Calories	542	
Total Fat	36.7g	47%
Saturated Fat	6.5g	33%
Cholesterol	81mg	27%
Sodium	251mg	11%
Total Carbohydrate	15.3g	6%
Dietary Fiber	5.1g	18%
Total Sugars	6.9g	
Protein	42.4g	

DESSERT RECIPES

Chocolate Barley Pudding

| Prep time: 10 min | Cook time: 30 min | Servings: 6 |

Ingredients

- ¾ cup uncooked barley
- 1 ¼ cups water
- 1 ½ cups unsweetened coconut milk
- ⅓ cup stevia
- 1 teaspoon vanilla extract
- ⅓ cup dried figs, unsweetened
- 1 tablespoon butter
- 2 tablespoons unsweetened cocoa

Directions

- Bring water to a boil in a saucepan.
- Stir the barley into a pan. Reduce the heat to low, cover, and cook for 20 minutes or until the barley is cooked through.
- Combine 1 1/2 cups cooked barley, milk, stevia, vanilla, dried figs, butter, and cocoa in the top of a double boiler over simmering water. Cook, stirring periodically, for 20 to 30 minutes, or until thickened.
- Pour into glasses or small bowls and serve hot or cold.

NUTRITION FACTS (PER SERVING)		
Calories	194	
Total Fat	3.2g	4%
Saturated Fat	1.9g	10%
Cholesterol	8mg	3%
Sodium	35mg	2%
Total Carbohydrate	39.1g	14%
Dietary Fiber	1.2g	4%
Total Sugars	17.9g	
Protein	3.6g	

Black Beans Chocolate Cake

Prep time: 15 min | Cook time: 40 min | Servings: 12

Ingredients

- *1 ½ cups semisweet chocolate chips*
- *1 (19 ounces) can of black beans, rinsed and drained*
- *4 eggs*
- *¾ cup stevia*
- *½ teaspoon baking powder*

Directions

- Preheat the oven to 350°F. Grease a 9-inch round cake pan.
- In a microwave-safe bowl, add the chocolate chips. Cook for about 2 minutes in the microwave, stirring every 20 seconds after the first minute until the chocolate is melted and smooth.
- In the bowl of a food processor, combine the beans and eggs. Blend until completely smooth. Pulse in the stevia and baking powder to combine. Pour in the melted chocolate and blend until smooth, scraping down the sides to ensure that the chocolate is evenly distributed. Place the batter in the cake pan that has been prepared.
- In a preheated oven, bake for 40 minutes or until golden.
- Cool for 10 to 15 minutes in the pan before inverting onto a serving platter.

NUTRITION FACTS (PER SERVING)

Calories	253	
Total Fat	5.2g	7%
Saturated Fat	1.2g	6%
Cholesterol	56mg	19%
Sodium	47mg	2%
Total Carbohydrate	43.6g	16%
Dietary Fiber	7.8g	28%
Total Sugars	18.1g	
Protein	10.8g	

Vanilla Cassava Flour Cupcakes

| Prep time: 15 min | Cook time: 20 min | Servings: 10 |

Ingredients

- ½ cup sesame oil
- ⅔ cup stevia
- ½ teaspoon salt
- 2 teaspoons vanilla extract
- 6 large eggs
- 2 tablespoons coconut milk
- ½ cup cassava flour
- 1 teaspoon baking powder

Directions

- Preheat oven to 350°F.

- Using 10 paper cupcake liners, line a 12-cup muffin tray. Grease the cupcake liners to ensure crumble-free cupcakes.
- Combine the oil, stevia, salt, vanilla, and eggs in a mixing bowl. Whisk in the milk until it is completely smooth.
- Sift together the cassava flour and baking powder in a separate bowl. Add the dry and wet ingredients in a mixing bowl, stirring to combine.
- Fill the liners 3/4 full with batter, then evenly distribute it among the 10 liners.
- Bake the cupcakes for 18 to 20 minutes on the center rack of the oven.
- Remove the cupcakes from the oven and cool for 5 minutes in the pan, then remove them from the pan and place them on a cooling rack.

NUTRITION FACTS (PER SERVING)

Calories	214	
Total Fat	14.7g	19%
Saturated Fat	3.1g	16%
Cholesterol	112mg	37%
Sodium	180mg	8%
Total Carbohydrate	17.5g	6%
Dietary Fiber	0.7g	2%
Total Sugars	13.2g	
Protein	3.9g	

Orange Cupcakes

| Prep time: 10 min | Cook time: 20 min | Servings: 12 |

Ingredients

- ⅝ cup unsweetened coconut milk
- 3 ¾ teaspoons orange juice
- ¼ cup sesame oil
- 2 egg whites, room temperature
- 2 oranges, zested
- 1 ½ teaspoons vanilla extract
- 1 ⅛ cups chickpeas flour
- ¾ cup stevia
- 2 teaspoons double-acting baking powder
- ¼ teaspoon salt

Directions

- Preheat the oven to 350°F. Line 12 muffin cups with paper liners or grease with a cooking spray.
- In a mixing bowl, add milk, orange juice, oil, egg whites, orange zest, and vanilla extract.
- In a large mixing basin, combine chickpeas flour, stevia, baking powder, and salt.
- Add the milk mixture to the flour mixture and beat on medium speed with an electric mixer for about 2 minutes, or until the batter is well combined. Fill lined muffin cups 3/4 full with batter.
- Bake for 18 to 20 minutes in a preheated oven, or until the tops are a light golden brown and a toothpick inserted in the center comes out clean. Cool for 10 minutes in the muffin tray before transferring to a wire rack to cool completely.

NUTRITION FACTS (PER SERVING)		
Calories	177	
Total Fat	7.3g	9%
Saturated Fat	1.8g	9%
Cholesterol	0mg	0%
Sodium	75mg	3%
Total Carbohydrate	25.9g	9%
Dietary Fiber	1.9g	7%
Total Sugars	19.7g	
Protein	3.3g	

Peach Balls

| Prep time: 15 min | Cook time: 0 min | Servings: 12 |

Ingredients

- ½ pound dried, unsweetened peaches
- ½ cup stevia
- ½ cup flaked coconut
- ½ (14 ounces) can (unsweetened) coconut milk
- 1 cup flaked coconut for rolling

Directions

- In a food processor, finely chop peaches. Toss with stevia in a mixing basin. Add the remaining ingredients and stir to combine.
- Form 1-inch balls and roll them in flaked coconut.
- Keep refrigerated until ready to use.

NUTRITION FACTS (PER SERVING)		
Calories	49	
Total Fat	1.6g	2%
Saturated Fat	1.4g	7%
Cholesterol	0mg	0%
Sodium	2mg	0%
Total Carbohydrate	9.2g	3%
Dietary Fiber	0.4g	1%
Total Sugars	8.8g	
Protein	0.2g	

Strawberry Clafoutis

| Prep time: 5 min | Cook time: 30 min | Servings: 8 |

Ingredients

- *3/4 cup strawberries*
- *1/2 cup flaxseed flour*
- *1/4 cup stevia*
- *4 eggs, lightly beaten*
- *1 cup hemp milk*
- *20g fruit puree, unsweetened*

Directions

- Preheat the oven to 350 °F. Grease a 22cm pie dish.
- Arrange strawberries in a single layer over the dish's base.
- Sift the flaxseed flour into a mixing basin and stir in the stevia.
- In a separate bowl, whisk together the eggs, hemp milk, and fruit puree.
- Gradually whisk the egg mixture into the flour until smooth. Bake for 30 minutes after pouring the batter over the strawberries.
- Remove from the oven, and serve right away.

NUTRITION FACTS (PER SERVING)

Calories	135	
Total Fat	4.1g	5%
Saturated Fat	0.8g	4%
Cholesterol	31mg	10%
Sodium	30mg	1%
Total Carbohydrate	18.3g	7%
Dietary Fiber	4.6g	16%
Total Sugars	0.7g	
Protein	7.5g	

Layered Raspberry Hemp Pudding

Prep time: 10 min   Cook time: 0 min   Servings: 2

Ingredients

- ½ cup raspberries
- 1 teaspoon pure vanilla extract
- 1 cup oat milk
- 1 tablespoon stevia
- 1/4 cup hemp seeds

Directions

- In a high-powered blender or food processor, combine the raspberries, vanilla, oat milk, and stevia and blend until smooth. Add the hemp seeds and pour into a glass or ceramic dish.
- Stir for 30 seconds, or until the hemp seeds begin to expand and are no longer dry on top or sinking to the bottom.
- Refrigerate for 4 hours or overnight, or until it achieves a thick pudding-like consistency.

NUTRITION FACTS (PER SERVING)

Calories	208	
Total Fat	13g	17%
Saturated Fat	3.7g	19%
Cholesterol	40mg	13%
Sodium	116mg	5%
Total Carbohydrate	17.6g	6%
Dietary Fiber	3.3g	12%
Total Sugars	8.5g	
Protein	5.9g	

Pears and Sunflower Seed Pancakes

Prep time: 10 min   Cook time: 10 min   Servings: 4

Ingredients

- *2 eggs*
- *1/3 cup hemp milk*
- *1 tablespoon sesame oil, melted*
- *1 tablespoon stevia, plus extra to serve*
- *1 ½ cups sunflower seed flour*
- *1 teaspoon baking powder*
- *½ cup grated pears, plus extra sliced to serve*
- *½ teaspoon ground nutmeg*

Directions

- Whisk together the eggs, milk, oil, and stevia in a large mixing basin.
- Combine sunflower seed flour, baking powder, pears grated, and nutmeg in a mixing bowl. Toss to blend thoroughly.
- Preheat a big nonstick frying pan over medium heat, lightly oiled. Pour 1/4 cups of batter into the pan in three batches.
- Cook the pancakes for 2-3 minutes, or until the surface bubbles and the bottom is golden brown. Cook for 1 minute on the other side.
- Serve with a dollop of Greek yogurt, more pears slices, and berries on top.

NUTRITION FACTS (PER SERVING)

Calories	282	
Total Fat	19.4g	25%
Saturated Fat	3.9g	20%
Cholesterol	41mg	14%
Sodium	149mg	6%
Total Carbohydrate	26.1g	9%
Dietary Fiber	1.6g	6%
Total Sugars	17.7g	
Protein	2.5g	

Chocolate Macadamia Nuts Cake

| Prep time: 15 min | Cook time: 40 min | Servings: 10 |

Ingredients

- ¼ cup unsalted butter
- 1 cup dark chocolate
- 1 cup macadamia nuts, roasted and ground
- 1 1/2 tbs cocoa
- 1 cup stevia
- 6 egg yolks
- 1 tsp vanilla extract
- 3 egg whites

Directions

- Preheat the oven to 350°F and grease the sides and base of the springform tin.
- In a saucepan, melt the butter and chocolate over low heat. Remove from the flame once melted.
- In a large mixing bowl, combine the macadamia nuts, cocoa, and stevia, reserving 2 tablespoons of stevia.
- Separate the eggs and add the 6 yolks to the chocolate mixture, along with the vanilla extract, and beat well.
- With an electric mixer, whip the egg whites until frothy, then add the leftover stevia and beat until glossy.
- In a large mixing bowl, combine the chocolate and macadamia nuts mixture, then fold in half of the egg whites gently.
- Carry on with the remaining egg whites in the same manner.
- Pour into a tin and bake for 40 minutes.
- Serve and enjoy!

NUTRITION FACTS (PER SERVING)

Calories	187	
Total Fat	14.4g	18%
Saturated Fat	3.5g	17%
Cholesterol	22mg	7%
Sodium	132mg	6%
Total Carbohydrate	10.6g	4%
Dietary Fiber	2.2g	8%
Total Sugars	7.3g	
Protein	5.1g	

Blueberry Flaxseed Cake

Prep time: 10 min   Cook time: 25 min   Servings: 6

Ingredients

- ½ cup butter softened
- 1/2 cup stevia
- 3 eggs
- 1 teaspoon lemon juice
- 1 lemon zested
- 1 cup flaxseed meal
- 1 cup sorghum flour
- 1/4 cup pecans
- 1 cup frozen blueberries

Directions

- Preheat the oven to 350°. Grease and greaseproof paper around 22cm springform baking tin.
- Cream the butter and stevia together until light and creamy. 1 at a time, add the eggs, beating well after each addition.
- With a big spoon or spatula, combine the lemon zest and juice. After that, fold in the flaxseed meal and sorghum flour.
- Spread the mixture evenly into the prepared baking tray. Place the blueberries and pecans on top of the cake mix and gently press them down.
- Bake for 30 minutes, or until golden brown and a skewer inserted in the center comes out clean.

NUTRITION FACTS (PER SERVING)		
Calories	280	
Total Fat	8.4g	11%
Saturated Fat	2.9g	14%
Cholesterol	51mg	17%
Sodium	38mg	2%
Total Carbohydrate	41.5g	15%
Dietary Fiber	8.4g	30%
Total Sugars	18.7g	
Protein	10.7g	

SMOOTHIES RECIPES

Fruity Smoothie

| Prep time: 10 min | Cook time: 0 min | Servings: 2 |

Ingredients

- *1 cup apricots*
- *½ dragon fruit, peeled and chopped*
- *1 cup unsweetened coconut milk*
- *1 tbsp hemp seeds*

Directions

- Place all ingredients in a high-speed blender.
- Blend until smooth.
- Serve and enjoy!

NUTRITION FACTS (PER SERVING)

Calories	352	
Total Fat	30.2g	39%
Saturated Fat	25.6g	128%
Cholesterol	0mg	0%
Sodium	21mg	1%
Total Carbohydrate	22.3g	8%
Dietary Fiber	6.2g	22%
Total Sugars	14.4g	
Protein	4.5g	

Smoothie with a Twist

Prep time: 10 min | Cook time: 0 min | Servings: 2

Ingredients

- *1 cup frozen raspberries, plus more for garnish*
- *1/2 cup frozen peach*
- *1/2 cup green apples, plus more for garnish*
- *1 cup hemp milk*

Directions

- Place all ingredients in a high-speed blender.
- Blend until smooth.
- Serve and enjoy!

NUTRITION FACTS (PER SERVING)

Calories	244	
Total Fat	3.8g	5%
Saturated Fat	0.4g	2%
Cholesterol	0mg	0%
Sodium	54mg	2%
Total Carbohydrate	51.7g	19%
Dietary Fiber	6.6g	24%
Total Sugars	45.7g	
Protein	3.7g	

Smoothie with Passion Fruit and Sunflower Butter

Prep time: 10 min | Cook time: 0 min | Servings: 2

Ingredients

- *2 tbsp pea protein*
- *1 banana*
- *1/2 cup passion fruit*
- *1 tbsp sunflower butter*
- *1/4 cup unsweetened oat milk*
- *1 cup ice*

Directions

- Place all ingredients in a high-speed blender.
- Blend until smooth.
- Serve and enjoy!

NUTRITION FACTS (PER SERVING)

Calories	498	
Total Fat	24.8g	32%
Saturated Fat	15.4g	77%
Cholesterol	65mg	22%
Sodium	147mg	6%
Total Carbohydrate	47.6g	17%
Dietary Fiber	7.1g	25%
Total Sugars	26.1g	
Protein	29.4g	

Beet Greens Smoothie

Prep time: 10 min Cook time: 0 min Servings: 1

Ingredients

- *1 cup beet greens chopped*
- *1 cup maple water*
- *1 cup ice*
- *1 small banana*
- *1/4 cup coconut milk*
- *1 tsp stevia*

Directions

- Place all ingredients in a high-speed blender.
- Blend until smooth.
- Serve and enjoy!

NUTRITION FACTS (PER SERVING)

Calories	207	
Total Fat	1.7g	2%
Saturated Fat	1.2g	6%
Cholesterol	4mg	1%
Sodium	327mg	14%
Total Carbohydrate	43.1g	16%
Dietary Fiber	5.9g	21%
Total Sugars	28.8g	
Protein	7.2g	

Goji Berries Smoothie

| Prep time: 10 min | Cook time: 0 min | Servings: 2 |

Ingredients

- *1 cup goji berries puree*
- *2 bananas*
- *1 cup grapefruit juice*
- *1 cup kiwi*
- *1 tbsp stevia*

Directions

- Place all ingredients in a high-speed blender.
- Blend until smooth.
- Serve and enjoy!

NUTRITION FACTS (PER SERVING)

Calories	246	
Total Fat	1g	1%
Saturated Fat	0.2g	1%
Cholesterol	0mg	0%
Sodium	41mg	2%
Total Carbohydrate	59.7g	22%
Dietary Fiber	8.5g	30%
Total Sugars	36.9g	
Protein	5g	

Raspberries, Chia, and Peanut Butter Smoothie

| Prep time: 10 min | Cook time: 0 min | Servings: 2 |

Ingredients

- *1 frozen peeled banana*
- *1/2 cup frozen raspberries*
- *1/4 cup unsweetened coconut milk*
- *1 tbsp peanut butter*
- *1 tbsp stevia*
- *1 cup water*
- *Sprinkle of salt*

Directions

- Place all ingredients in a high-speed blender.
- Blend until smooth.
- Serve and enjoy!

NUTRITION FACTS (PER SERVING)

Calories	335	
Total Fat	10.1g	13%
Saturated Fat	1.4g	7%
Cholesterol	4mg	1%
Sodium	208mg	9%
Total Carbohydrate	58.1g	21%
Dietary Fiber	6.2g	22%
Total Sugars	41.2g	
Protein	8.2g	

Green Apples & Citrus Smoothie

Prep time: 10 min   Cook time: 0 min   Servings: 2

Ingredients

- ¾ cup orange juice blend
- ¼ cup parsnips juice
- 1 cup green apple chunks
- ½ banana

Directions

- Place all ingredients in a high-speed blender.
- Blend until smooth.
- Serve and enjoy!

NUTRITION FACTS (PER SERVING)

Calories	277	
Total Fat	1.1g	1%
Saturated Fat	0.2g	1%
Cholesterol	0mg	0%
Sodium	7mg	0%
Total Carbohydrate	69.6g	25%
Dietary Fiber	8.9g	32%
Total Sugars	47.6g	
Protein	2.9g	

Nectarines Smoothie

Prep time: 10 min   Cook time: 0 min   Servings: 2

Ingredients

- *2/3 cup frozen nectarines*
- *1/2 cup chopped zucchini*
- *1/4 cup unsweetened coconut water*
- *toasted coconut chips for serving*

Directions

- Place all ingredients in a high-speed blender.
- Blend until smooth.
- Sprinkle with coconut chips is desired.
- Serve and enjoy!

NUTRITION FACTS (PER SERVING)

Calories	61	
Total Fat	0.5g	1%
Saturated Fat	0.2g	1%
Cholesterol	0mg	0%
Sodium	69mg	3%
Total Carbohydrate	13.8g	5%
Dietary Fiber	2.8g	10%
Total Sugars	9.8g	
Protein	2.1g	

Matcha Smoothie

| Prep time: 10 min | Cook time: 0 min | Servings: 2 |

Ingredients

- 1 1/2 cup matcha tea
- 2 cup blueberries
- 1 sliced banana
- 3 tbsp stevia

Directions

- Place all ingredients in a high-speed blender.
- Blend until smooth.
- Serve and enjoy!

NUTRITION FACTS (PER SERVING)		
Calories	257	
Total Fat	1.4g	2%
Saturated Fat	0.1g	0%
Cholesterol	0mg	0%
Sodium	20mg	1%
Total Carbohydrate	63g	23%
Dietary Fiber	5g	18%
Total Sugars	48.6g	
Protein	2.2g	

Pears, Turnips & Red Cabbage Smoothie

| Prep time: 10 min | Cook time: 0 min | Servings: 2 |

Ingredients

- ¼ red cabbage chopped
- 1 pear, cut into 2-inch chunks
- 3 turnips, ends trimmed, cut into 2-inch chunks
- 1 lemon, juiced
- 1 2-inch piece fresh ginger, peeled
- 1 cup cold water

Directions

- Place all ingredients in a high-speed blender.
- Blend until smooth.
- Serve and enjoy!

NUTRITION FACTS (PER SERVING)

Calories	111	
Total Fat	0.3g	0%
Saturated Fat	0g	0%
Cholesterol	0mg	0%
Sodium	129mg	6%
Total Carbohydrate	27.4g	10%
Dietary Fiber	6.4g	23%
Total Sugars	15.5g	
Protein	2.4g	

2-WEEKS MEAL PLAN

1st Week

Day	Breakfast	Snack	Lunch	Dinner	Dessert
1	Hazelnuts Pancakes	Matcha Smoothie	One Pot Pork & Pepper Stew	Raisins Cider Pork	Layered Raspberry Hemp Pudding
2	Baby Kale Omelette	Raspberries, Chia and Peanut Butter Smoothie	Scallops & Avocado Salad	Hemp & Basil Scallops	Strawberry Clafoutis
3	Rutabaga Pancakes	Smoothie with Passion Fruit and Sunflower Butter	Grilled Beef with Pesto	Black Beans, Kale and Barley Patties	Blac Beans Chocolate Cake
4	Hemp Seed Porridge	Eggplant Waffles	Garlicky Lime Halibut	Garlic Cilantro Crabmeat	Vanilla Cassava Flour Cupcakes
5	Sorghum Breakfast Pudding	Pears, Turnips & Red Cabbage Smoothie	Zucchini Lasagna	Creamy Avocado Orange Trout	Blueberry Flaxseed Cake
6	Parsnips Barley Muffins	Goji Berries Smoothie	Cranberry Beans & Pork Chili	Peaches & Carrot Teff	Orange Cupcakes
7	Quinoa & Flax Porridge	Green Apples & Citrus SMoothie	Peach Chutney Lamb Curry	Pine Nuts Baked Mackerel	Pears & Sunflower Seed Pancakes

2nd Week

Day	Breakfast	Snack	Lunch	Dinner	Dessert
1	Chickpeas Flour Pancakes	Fruity Smoothie	Cranberry Beans & Pork Chili	Pine Nuts Baked Mackerel	Blueberry Flaxseed Cake
2	Beet Greens Asparagus Quiche Cups	Smoothie with a Twist	Sardines Salad	Northern Beans Soup	Chocolate Macadamia Nuts Cake
3	Hazelnuts Pancakes	Goji Berries Smoothie	Turkey & Flax Seeds Salad	Raisins Cider Pork	Vanilla Cassava Flour Cupcakes
4	Eggplant Waffles	Smoothie with Passion Fruit and Sunflower Butter	Grilled Beef with Pesto	Hemp & Basil Scallops	Chocolate & Barley Pudding
5	Hemp Seed Porridge	Nectarines Smoothie	One Pot Pork & Pepper Stew	Garlic Cilantro Crabmeat	Strawberry Clafoutis
6	Parsnips Barley Muffins	Matcha Smoothie	Garlicky Lime Halibut	Balsamic Vinegar Glazed Beef	Orange Cupcakes
7	Baby Kale Omelette	Quinoa & Flax Porridge	Jerk Lamb	Pine Nuts Baked Mackerel	Peach Balls